EVOLUTION

of a

POET

TRANZZII GEE

Print information available on the last page

Rev. date: 04/23/2019

To order additional copies of this book, contact:
Xlibris
1-800-455-039
www.xlibris.com.au
Orders@Xlibris.com.au

"Your beliefs become your thoughts,
Your thoughts become your words,
Your words become your actions,
Your actions become your habits,
Your habits become your values,
Your values become your destiny."

Gandhi

GUILTY

Guilt is not something,
That can be sustained.
It gnaws and it eats,
Til blood stains remain.
It bleeds you,
And drains you.
Til nothing is left.
Nothing alive,
Just dead rotting flesh.
It becomes a disease.
And you painfully moan.
You bite and you groan.
And share it all round.
No friends.
They're all gone.
Now you're alone,
No one to bemoan.
No one to share in your pain.
Desires are gone.
No love can you feel.
Emotionless wreck You've become.
Devouring souls,
Of those who would love you..
Unfeeling and dead,
Your hunger will never be fed…

TRANZZII GEE
15/04/2018

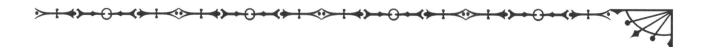

Everybody says they know...
Good from bad,
And right from wrong.
Then continue,
with their petty ways,
That they grew so used to over time.
Believing they are good.
Deluded by the self...
Never seeing truth,
Hidden by the self.
Never seeing the harm they do...
How can they not i ask...
A blind eye turned upon themselves.
Mindful never enters in,
Unless it profits them.
Caring only for themselves,
And what they have to gain...
Profit gained emotionally,
Not all gain is monetary.
Riches stored within the heart,
Are riches of great worth.
From these are borne,
The things of love.
The things that feed the soul.
The things that being mindful brings.
These things feed the soul.
Not things of dark...
Not secrets kept...
Not greed nor hate...
Nor guilt...

Those things,
They bring the soul,
The things it never wants.
Bring instead the things it wants
The things of of love and light.
Those things that bring the smiles,
Of absolute delight.
Dwell on love...
And dwell on life...
Dream the dreams.
Make them big.
And dwell on those instead.
A promise here i make to you,
Regrets will fall away,
And in their place,
A seed of joy,
will germinate within,
And the tree,
Of joy will grow.
That tree once grown,
Will never die.
And life will feel complete.

MORE FROM
TRANZZII GEE

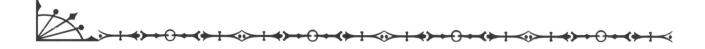

EVOLUTION OF A POET

I did one day,
Begin to write,
Some words
I put on paper.
It really wasn't very good,
Made no sense at all.
The night my brother died.
I wrote another one
It said it all to me,
And to all his friends.
It made em laugh and made cry.
No dry eyes to be seen.
It made them feel,
It made them know
The man i knew he was.
Then it got lost within the void,
The void we all call life.
I like to think he took it.
Cos it was just for him.
T'was many many years,
Before another one presented to my mind.
I wrote it down and hated it.
Into a ball it turned.
The distance in between each one
Grew and grew and grew,
Til i was sure another one,

Would never come again.
Years went by and nothing came.
I never really cared.
For me my dreams,
Were never meant,
To be acheived.
A big mistake was made.
Now im writing everyday,
Inspired by events,
That come and go within my life.
With quite some frequency.
So never quit,
The things you dream,
You never know just when.
Things will turn about.
And life will change,
Your dreams will come about.
Never leave your hope behind.
Or forget to love each day.
Cos life can change so suddenly.
And your dreams will come about.

TRANZZII GEE
15/04/2018

I look to the sky,
When i am sad.
I see your smile,
In the sun,
As it shines on me.
Amplified beauty,
The beautiful you.
Lifting me up,
To where i belong.
To be in your light,
Thats all that i need.
To see you smiling each day.
To talk and to joke,
And be silly sometimes.
To bask in the warmth,
Of the gold that is you.
Your smile brings me such joy,
Like nothing before.
Nothing compares,
To the gold that is you.
And id share with you,
The love that is me.
No more would i need...
In my life...
Just you...

TRANZZII GEE
16TH MARCH 2018

Focus on your dreams.
On what you want to be.
On who you would become.
Happiness is there for you.
Just focus on the one.
The one who is within the you...
That one who is you.
The one who matters most to you,
Or should...
Be the one you want to be,
Not what others want.
Happiness is there for you.
Be just who you want…

TRANZZII GEE 19/04/2018

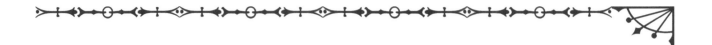

Let me pull you up,
When you are feeling sad.
Or feeling low as well.
And you can do
the same for me.
The times that i am down.
Lifes to short,
For feeling bad.
Be true to who you are.
A being of light,
And wondrous gifts.
Share it all around.
That which dwells in each of us.
Each and all of us.
Wants to let you to feel the love,
Each of you should know by now,
Nothing's as it seems.
Nothing here is true at all.
When eyes of love are used.
Hate just burns and sears.
Torturing to tears.
While love is warm,
And comfort gives.
Like scented flowers borne.
Find the love you have within.
Listen to the voice that calls....
The love within you all

TRANZZII GEE
18/04/2018

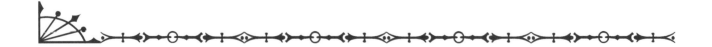

MADNESS

Madness creeping in...
Insanity within...
Twisting in my mind,
Like a living thing.
Which ways up?
Which ways down?
Left and right confused.
Something writhing inside out.
Coming from the depths of me.
My life has turned itself,
Completely upside down and Inside out.
All the walls are stripped away.
Nothing to conceal,
The me i really am.
Born a boy,
My heart a girl,
My mind a twisted knot.
Its plain to see if you look.
Im just not what I seem.
There's more to me,
You'll never know,
For you refuse look.
These depths are deeper,
Than would dare to go.
Dont be scared to dive.
Theres nothing there to fear.
But no one dares to go down there.
And find out who i am.

TRANZZII GEE
20/04/2018.

Realised very recently,
Nothing really matters.
The works of man,
The things they do.
All the shit they think is true.
None of what they think is real,
Nothing really matters.
A song i heard long ago,
That is a favoured tune.
Tells the truth of how it is,
And how it oughta be.
Get in touch with ya self.
To have a life of glee.
Cos in the end,
When all is done,
And all is said,
Nothing else matters.
So thanks to james,
And all the band.
They call emselves metallica.
The truth to you they'll tell,
In all ya songs.
Is plain for me to see
Like a moth into the fame
Im almost there.
Cya when im done.
Ive got a lot to tell.

TRANZZII GEE
25/04/2018

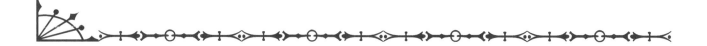

Standing now.
Facing east.
Predawn cold bites my cheeks.
I shiver in anticipation,
Of the rising of the sun.
I see the glow of coming dawn.
Shadows start to flee.
The shape of things are forming.
All the things of truth,
Im free.
As shadows flee.
No more lies,
within my mind.
All the monsters flee.
The darkness of my life,
Gone from inside me.
The wings i never knew i had unfurl.
And spread.
It fills me with delight.
I lift into the sky.
And fly toward the sun,
I like a moth into the flame.
To be consumed.
And be as one.
With who i really am.

TRANZZII GEE
25/04/2018

Dead eye joes,
They're all around.
Look into their eyes.
But dont be fooled,
Some look alive.
They're just the walking dead.
They'll grab and grasp.
And bite at you,
They want what's in your head.
They lack a soul.
No care have they.
They wish you be like them.
Beware of dead eye joe's.
They'll kill your joy.
And bring you down,
They care not how.
They want you just like them.
Dead eye joe consumes and takes,
Til nothings left in within.
They'll suck you dry.
Of all the love,
That you ever felt,
Don't get caught by dead joe,
Destruction is assured.
Run away and don't look back.
Dead eye joe pursues.
They think you owe them dues.
Dead eye joes,
They think they know.
What life is all about.
But dead is all they know.
So run i beg.
Run right now...
Dead eyes on the prowl....

TRANZZII GEE
25/04/2018

10

END OF DAY LAMENT

Its time now,
I just gave up.
My day of struggle and strife,
I kept that smile on me face.
Minute by minute...
And hour by hour...
I kept that fucker in place.
Everytime it tried to hide.
I beat its fuckin arse.
Get back i screamed at the fuck,
You're not done just yet.
There's five more goddam hours.
Get back in place i screamed.
And dont you dare hide again.
Ill slap ya fucken face.
I smiled through the fuckheads,
Out on them roads,
The old bitch,
In the carpark at woollies.
And now the fuckin sun's has gone down.
My smile just wont go,
Cos i just fucken realised...
I made it through the day...
And that was one fucked up day.
So anyone tryin' to read,
The shit ive written here.
Smile before you go ta bed...
Cos you made it to, you hear?

TRANZZII GEE
26/04/2018

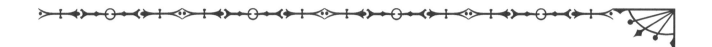

THE HUNGER

I hunger for your mind.
To embrace your soul with mine.
I hunger for the things i see,
When i look into your eyes.
I hunger for your voice.
To hear your words,
Caress my ears,
Like summers ocean breeze.
To feel your touch,
Upon my skin.
As you rest your hand in mine.
My hunger is for you.
I hunger for your lips,
Pressed firm against my own.
To taste your breathe,
And feel that i am home.
I hunger for the whole of you.
Not just what is seen.
I hunger for your souls embrace.
Interlocked with mine.

TRANZZII GEE
07/05/2018

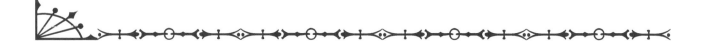

USTOPPABLE

I feel a little different now,
Like things are falling into place,
The cards are on the table,
There is but one left there to turn.
I know the hands a winner,
I have no doubts it is.
Just waiting on the dealer,
To show her hand to me.
The time she takes is up to her.
She won't be pushed on time.
And the timings always perfect.
No mistakes by her are made.
The sweat is on my brow.
Nerves all strung fairly tight,
Like strings on a guitar.
But i know ive got a winner here.
Now i feel the love inside,
Welling up from deep within,
Ready to explode.
For everyone to see.
I never thought i'd make it through.
The shit that i just did.
Manic swinging left and right.
Never balanced never true,
This is what the world comes to,
When it's time for meeting you.
A tide that can't be stopped.
Beating 'gainst the rocks.

TRANZZII GEE
10/05/2018

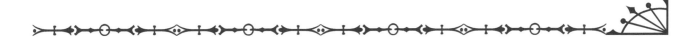

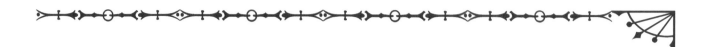

ITS GOTTA GIVE

I know that somethings gotta give,
Somethings gotta break.
Or ill never leave this cage im in,
The one i made myself.
I stepped on in,
And closed the door.
Then threw away the key.
I made it strong i did.
I made it not to bend.
Something now,
Has to break.
Release may never come.
Third time round is this for me
Ive gotta make a break.
For one more time,
Might kill my soul.
Then it wouldnt end.
Stuck right here in hell,
For all eternity.
Heaven calls.
Ive gotta go.
Ive gotta make a break for it.
For hell is not a place for me,

To live eternally.
Ive gotta make a break for it,
And find my angel here.
My angel is my way to heaven.
With me eternally.
Ive gotta make break for it.
Will someone come and help?
Ive gotta make a break for it.
Or die eternally.
Heaven calls,
The trumpets sound.
Heralding the help i need,
Is about to come.
Where now is my angel gone?
I need her most right now.
Where now is my angel gone?
Out there in the world.
I call out to my angel now,
Its almost time to come....

TRANZZII GEE
12/05/2018

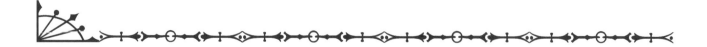

FOR MY DAD

What is there that i can say,
About the hero who is my dad.
Not sure there's really any words,
Strong enough to say.
I'll start and say,
I love you now,
Just as much as when i was young.
It always seemed you were there for me,
Whenever that you could.
You accepted all the stupid things,
I did when i was young
Mostly with a smile.
But even when i made you mad,
It never lasted long.
You took me here,
And took me there,
Places others never went.
Made sure that i experienced,
Everything i could.
I just wanted to write this down,
To let you know just how much,
I appreciate it all.,
Everything you've ever done,
And tell you of the love….
This kid has for her dad.

TRANZZII GEE
16/05/2018

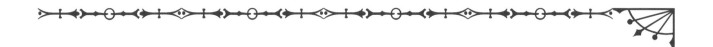

WHEN ANGELS CALL

Will you heed.
What they say to you.
Will you seek and find,
The freedom offered unto you.
Or will you to stay in hell.
Tortured unto death.
Unto death until you die.
And repeat it all again.
Back and forth,
Tidal flows.
Which way will you go.
Unto death or free in life.
The end is up to you.
What will you do when angels call.
And madness starts again.
Heed the call it ebbs and flows,
Back and forth.
Choose that which you will.
Do not miss your chance this time.
The end begins anew.

TRANZZII GEE
28/05/2018

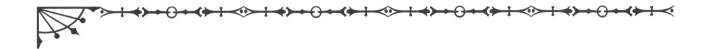

NEVERMORE

Never again,
Shall i be.
Shackled unto tyranny.
By piece of paper.
Shackle bound.
Unto death so bound.
Nevermore.
Shall i trade.
My dreams for nothing more,
Than empty oaths and promises.
Words that have no worth.
Forever more.
I will seek.
I will find.
I will surely have,
Spirit bound.
No promises.
No emptiness.
Fullness found.
In silence bound.
A love unfound.
In silence bound.
No words describe.
What i have found.
Embraced and held,
In silence bound.
Something so profound.
This for you to understand.
Never more shall i be bound.
By emptiness and lies.

TRANZZII GEE
28/05/2018.

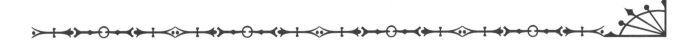

CHANGE

My mind...
Feels like its melting.
Melting and remoulding,
Into something new.
Something me.
Something free.
Something new for me.
Not changing me.
Nor changing who i am.
Just changing how i look at things.
Making me,
The me i am,
The me i always was.
Not the me i made,
To hide meself behind.
This new me,
As it turns out,
Was always me inside.
Do not worry bout the change.
You may see in me.
Its the better me,
The nicer me.
The me i always was.
The original was always best.
Not the me i made.

TRANZZII GEE
28/05/2018.

WHERE AM I

Where shines the light,
When no light shines on me.
I chase the light within,
But no light shines on me.
I travel this world alone.
No friends do walk with me.
In darkness doomed eternally?
Yet still i chase the light in me.
I walk the empty paths,
In darkness i do stumble,
Sometimes to fall,
Then to crawl,
On hand and bended knee.
To chase the light i see in me.
No longer is my worth defined.
By unrefined,
And worthless things,
Found externally.
My worth comes now,
From deep within.
Darkness pauses.
Shadows shift.
As darkness now declines.
The light now grows in strength.
The shadows flee.
The light does shine,
The dawn of a new day begins.
The sun does rise within.
My soul it does rejoice.
The has dawned.
Priceless now am i.

TRANZZII GEE
31/05/2018

Like a wildfire,
Consuming what i am.
Devouring whats left of me.
Leaving ash behind.
Then just like the pheonix.
Rising from its seeming death.
Risen from the grave,
Risen from the depths of hell.
Freedom now is found.
Setting foot on hidden paths.
Never more be blind.
With each and every passing day.
Strength returns...
Vision clears...
Never more be bound,
By ways of wicked man.
Risen now above the strife,
No more bound to earthly life.
Heav'n bound on wings aflame.
Free now...
Never bound...

TRANZZII GEE
31052018

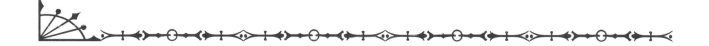

WITHIN YOU

Within your eyes,.
Eternity.
Cosmic shift,
I see the angels sing…
Within your eyes,
Your soul does dance,
To the echoes of your dreams.
Within your eyes,
Sadness born,
Scars of lost love healed.
Within your eyes,
Love is borne,
Held eternally.
Within your eyes,
The soft caress,
Of summers cooling breeze.
Within your eyes,
I see the stars,
And galaxies,
Spin slowly,
Endlessly.
Within your eyes,
A love i see,
Borne of the moon,
And deepest sea,
A love so deep and real.
Within your eyes I see you.
The you, You are become…

TRANZZII GEE
02/01/2018

JADED

Fading into oblivion,
No idea how to halt this flow.
My mind grows dim,
My heart it yearns,
For anything to show.
Im tired of waking up alone,
No one there to give my love…
Im tired of living life in fear,
Im tired of not living.
But i thank my god,
For all my friends,
That make my life worth something.

TRANZZII GEE
19/11/2018

NO COMPRISE

Would you hold my hand,
Were I there with you,
Would hold me in your arms?
Would tell me all the things,
I need to hear from you?
Would you love me,
With no compromise,
No guilt nor lies,
Just open truth?
Would you tell me,
All the things you feel,
The things from deep inside?
I know you're there,
And reading this,
Don't deny the things you feel,
The one who'll be life.

TRANZZII GEE
04/11/2018

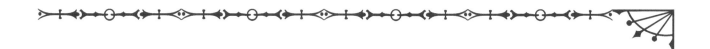

CHANGES

Follow now the siren sound,
Whisper in the wind,
Watch now as change comes round,
A lightness in your head.
Walk the path that darkness bled,
Paved with souls,
All damned by time,
The light glows up ahead.
I survived to live and love
I am born again,
The darkest now all bled away,
The light grows strong within.

TRANZZII GEE
30/10/2018

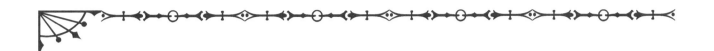

I KNEW YOU

I knew I knew you,
even fore i ever knew,
Now I find I know you here.
In secret places,
Spirits dwell,
These places feel like heav'n.
There's nothing else,
This place could be,
With you in my life.

TRANZZII GEE
27/10/2018

INDIGO LIGHT

I travel now,
Within the light,
This child of indigo.
This light within,
That shines so bright,
So much brighter than before…
No gray, No black…
Just shades of blue and indigo,
Let my soul shine bright.

TRANZZII GEE
27/10/2018

THE COSMOS SINGS

You know the cosmos sings,
Tune of creation told,
It speaks to my old soul,
It renews me to my core.
You know the tune within,
Or does discord block the sound?
Let the tune renew,
Let your soul be found.
You know you feel it to,
The tune you hear within'.
You feel it in your heart,
If you just turn within'.
Discord comes undone,
As angel voices heard.
Angelic souls recommune,
And your soul is heard.
Don't let the discord maim.
Nor disconnect you from your soul
Just let the discord go,
And feel your peace within....

TRANZZII GEE
25/10/2018

PERCEPTIONS CHANGE

Perceptions change,
Beliefs,…
They fade…
Positive energies flow.
Success achieved,
Some small…
Some big…
In the details all around.
Vision clears…
I see things now,
I've never seen before…
Redemption won,
Before the throne,
The universe it cheers.

TRANZZII GEE
24/10/2018

MY ETERNAL FLAME

live in different worlds,
Though our souls are bound,
Both the same.
Eternal flame….
You are part of me I'm sure.
I wish that you,
Were in my life,
To hold you in my arms…
A beacon lit,
A ray of light,
My eternal flame.

TRANZZII GEE
22/10/2018

MAYBE

Maybein another time,
Another life maybe,
Things are different,
There for us,
We're one,
Not two,
Like here.
One of mind,
Of spirit to,
Heart beats synched,
As one.

TRANZZII GEE
21/10/2018
October 21, 2018 0 Edit Post

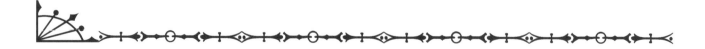

UPON THE BEACH

I waited there upon the beach,
To see what never comes.
I stood there ankle deep,
The waves they lapped around.
I stared out there past the break,
Hoping i would see.
Hoping i would see,
That that's never seen.
Hoping she would take me home,
There beneath the sea.

TRANZZII GEE
20/10/2018

I'M DONE

I wish to say goodbye cruel world,
I have had enough of you.
But here I'm stuck,
Learning how,
To get to know myself.
I'm done with life,
And growing up.
I'm done with friends,
Who are not friends,
I'm done with life alone.
Pretty much I'm done with this,
And the way it makes me feel.
I've had enough of feeling things,
That truly can't be real,
Everything for me it seems is just impossible.

TRANZZII GEE
19/10/2018

ITS AN ILLUSION

Its all just illusion,
All you think you know.
So many different realities,
So many different worlds.
What's real?
What's not?
Can you please define it?
Each and every one,
Will say its something else.
Define for me,
What love might be,
Or hate or passion,
Or simple desire,
In the end what it is,
Its all just frequency.
What is real and what is not?
The whisper in your mind?
The feeling in your heart?
Spirit bred,
Emotion fed,
What's real and what is not?

TRANZZII GEE
16/10/2018

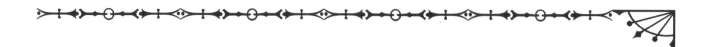

SIRENS SONG

The stars they sing,
The planets dance,
To creations tune.
Creation sings,
Her siren song,
All of man are drawn.
To hear the song,
Creation sings,
And understand the words.
Eyes all drawn,
Heavenward,
So few will look within.
For answers,
Hidden secretly,
Within the minds man.

TRANZZII GEE
15/10/2018
October 15, 2018 0 Edit Post

MY WISH TO

I find me wishing,
Wishing for a world,
Where violence didn't live.
A world of peace…
A world of love…
A world where no ones scared…
A world where people lend a hand,
Not a fist or violent word.
Let me count the hands,
Of those who would agree.
I find me wishing,
Wishing for a world,
Where violence doesn't live.
No war nor hate.
No intolerance for someone's race.
No hate for different points of view.
A world where people stop and think,
Before they spew their words of hate.
I find me wishing,
Wishing for a world,
Where violence cannot live.

TRANZZII GEE
11/10/2018

BE KIND

Be kind,
Be kind to your cat,
Be kind to your dog,
Be kind to your budgie as well.
Be kind to the rudeness,
Encountered in life,
Be kind to your enemies to,
Be kind to the asshole,
Livin' next door…
Be kind to one down the street…
Choose to be kind,
And change someone's day,
I believe,
It will change yours as well.
But most of all…
Above all the rest…
Just be kind to yourself.

TRANZZII GEE
10/10/2018

AS IN A DREAM

So many people living in fear,
Fear of what others will think.
What would they think,
If i was honest with them.
And told them men are for me.
What would they think,
If i was honest with them,
And told em i like women as well.
What would they think,
If i presented as me.
A man on the outside,
Woman within…
Scared to be seen,
For ridicule brings,
I'm just being honest with you.
Would you be shy,
To be seen by my side,
Walking the streets in a dress?
I'm just asking,
Be honest with me.
And more so,
Be honest with self.
Stop living in fear,
Of what others may think,
So many delusions out there.
Thinking things are,
The way they are not,
Believing the lies,
They help spread.
So often there's proof,
Things aren't what they seem,
But no one will bother to look.
It brings so much comfort,
Just believing you're right,
living your life in a lie…
Like I did.
Living my life as if in a dream.

TRANZZII GEE
08/10/2018

WHAT A DREAM

What a dream i just had.
It was weird as can be.
From the start
To the curious end.
The starts not important,
It's the end that stands out…
I met a man,
An oldish man,
Who sat down like dog,
The cutest dog was he.
He was blue as he was grey,
But the most curious thing,
Was he had a dick that spoke.
The penis' mouth wasn't small,
Like you'd think it would…
It was big,
Like that of a frog.
And the jokes that it told,
The things that it said,
I laughed so hard that I died.
When I awoke,
I wrote this all down,
So you could chuckle like me.

TRANZZII GEE
05/0/2018

BIT BY BIT

Bit by bit,
I think I can.
Bit by bit,
I grow each day.
Bit by bit,
I climb this hill.
Bit by bit
I'm higher still.
Bit by bit,
I won't fall down.
Bit by bit,
I am known.
Bit by bit,
I know myself.
Bit by bit,
I'll win this game.
Then bit by bit,
I'll come back down,
And bit by bit,
I'll lend a hand.
So bit by bit,
You know you can.

TRANZZII GEE
05/10/2018

WE MET BUT ONCE

My love of you,
Wont go away,
We met but once,
So long ago…
With a hug,
You lit me up inside,
Opened something,
Deep within…
That door you opened oh so wide,
Will never close to you,
No matter how you try,
I only hope you feel,
The same as what i do,
You have to feel its true for you
Or it can never be…
It stands so wide,
But only you,
Will ever enter it,
No one else can pass within,
'Cos you do hold the key.
I never dreamed,
I never hoped,
I never thought,
That this could be…
I knew it then,
As i walked away,
Still I feel the same…
But so much stronger now…
And if I'm wrong,
Then so be it,
I'll spend my life alone.

TRANZZII GEE
01/10/2018

FOREVER AGO

Forever ago,
Looking back.
And how we met,
When we were born.
At inception,
When our souls came forth,
We were one,
Then two as well.
And now,
How we met again,
Seems so impossible.
In this place,
And in this time.
Am I insane in this?
Now looking forward,
To what is yet to come.
I cannot see a future,
Without you in it too.

TRANZZII GEE
28/09/2018

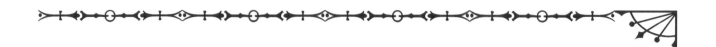

TWIN FLAME

Twin flame of mine,
Two souls entwine.
Your fears are felt,
Your pain is mine.
Your hope,
Your joy,
Are mine to share,
As mine are there for you.
The trust I feel I have in you,
Never known before.
Intimate like nothing else,
Ever felt on earth.

TRANZZII GEE
26/09/2018

WASTED WAR

Slowly it devolved,
Bit by little bit,
Piece by tiny piece it went,
Never to return…
The me I made,
To hide away,
The life that I made to please,
The others in my life…
I never knew what happy was,
Til it all went away,
The turmoil came into my life,
I fought for what I had…
I fought the battle,
Lost the war,
The war,
That was within…
I look back now and see it clear,
If I had just surrendered,
Surrendered then unto myself,
And my every whim…
Now my life,
Almost complete,
Brings happiness and joy,
I'm looking back no more…

TRANZZII GEE
25/09/2018

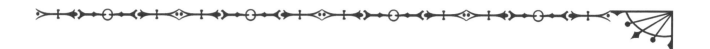

PASSION

With a passion unmatched,
She lived her life,
In passion dwelt,
With passion lived,
Yesterday never was,
Tomorrow never comes,
Living passion in the now.
With passion loved,
And lifted up,
With passion she was felled,
Then lifted up in arms of love,
They lived their lives,
Passion held,
Embraced in love.
Divinity was theirs,
And with the gods they dwell.

TRANZZII GEE
25/09/2018

APOCALYPSE

Apocalypse for me is now,
Truth revealed,
Curtains rend,
Veils ripped away…
The truth of who I once was,
Revealed in hearts and spades.
What I am has come again,
Not what I was,
But who I was before.
My heart now knows,
What truth is there,
The heart,
What truth,
Cannot divine..?
Feel what truth there is for you,
Within your heart you know.
Don't deny what lays down there,
Deep within your soul.

TRANZZII GEE
25/09/2018

PERFECT

Perfectly me,
Imperfectly done,
Perfect for who I'm become…
Perfectly imperfect,
In what makes up me,
Perfection a lie to begin…
Now I can see,
Perfection in you,
Imperfectly perfect its true…

TRANZZII GEE
25/09/2018

THE DREAM

I lived my life like in a dream,
Nothing really mattered.
I waited so long for it to end,
But death ignored my plea.
Nightmare was reality,
By day and by night.
Dawn the darkest light.
My reality.
Wake me then when its all done
Wake me when its over.
Wake me from this walking death,
That rules inside my head.
I prayed then to the god i knew,
The god inside of me.
Waking now eternal flame,
The light has changed in me.

TRANZZII GEE
26/09/2018

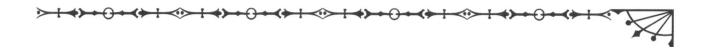

YOURS

I am yours,
You are mine.
True since time began…
I am she,
You are my he.
Entwined and bound are we…
Eternity is no more time,
For the time i want with you.
Eternal made am i for you,
You were made for me…
Eternally,
We exist,
Within each others arms.

TRANZZII GEE
25/09/2018

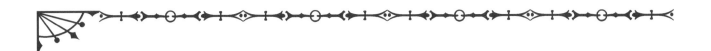

GREAT DIVIDE

Across the great divide i see,
Chasms wide and mountain peaks.
The journey seems impossible,
But for the distance i have come.
I stand and stare in awe,
At the vista spread before.
The beauty of the world we're in,
Had escaped my eye til then.
Standing here right beside,
This chasm open wide.
Vertigo ascends inside,
I want to spread my wings.

TRANZZII GEE
25/09/2018

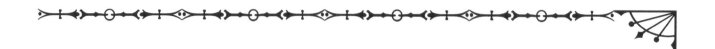

BOUND

Bind now my soul to me,
Come join me like you should.
Come join me here and here will be,
Our home throughout eternity,
Then shall this journey start,
Here now in this realm of ours.
Bound now once for all,
Bind my mind to thine.
And be with me,
Through all eternity.

CHANGE

Its time for a change,
Old ways are done.
They simply do not work,
Chasms wide,
Division sides.
So many problems,
In people's lives.
The world we knew,
When we were young,
Like innocence now lost and done,
The world has gone completely mad.
War for profit it's so sad…
Killin' kids with drugs called meds…
People thinkin' its for them,
Thinkin' they're all safe in bed…
Cons and lies is all it is…
I think it's time you used your head…
Waking up is hard to do,
When drugged on drunken lies…
Stagger to…
Stagger fro…
Spin them all around…
No one knows which way is up…
And then they all fall down.
Governments not in control,
As bankers laugh and charge a toll…
The one percent control the world,
The ninety nine are never told…
The time has come for making smiles…
Breeding love…
Contented lives…
The time of change is almost here…
This era of disease is done.

TRANZZII GEE
22/09/2018

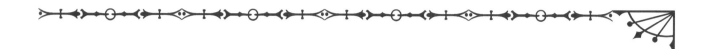

WOULD YOU...

Would you tear down perfection,
To rebuild it a new.
To make it,
More beautiful to you?
Take what you knew,
And make it all new.
In way you can now understand,
And accept?
Would you tear down perfection,
On a chance and a whim,
That that it could be better,
than anything past,
That you knew?

TRANZZII GEE
21/09/2018

LET ME SLEEP

Let me sleep,
Long and sweet.
Let me lay,
Where angels weep.
Wrapped within,
That warm embrace.
Enfolded in her wings,
At peace…..

TRANZZII GEE
18/09/2018

MY EYES ARE CLOSED

My eyes are closed,
yet no sleep comes.
I see them there,
like sleeping drones.
My eyes are closed,
To what really is.
I see what really is,
When my eyes are closed.
I see me there,
When my eyes are closed.
Why cant I stay,
Where my eyes are closed.

TRANZZII GEE
18/19/2018

THE END

I'll try not to let you down,
Try to love you more.
I'm sorry I forgot you,
In all life's ups n downs.
It was never my intent,
To leave you by the way.
Never meant ignoring you,
But it became my way.
I never meant for anything,
To come between us then.
Now it all seems to late,
To put it on the mend.
This is all just so damned hard,
Each and everyday.
I never meant for it to be like this,
This close to the end.

TRANZZII GEE
16/09/2018

THIS IS MY HELL

Once i had dreams,
They are gone with my hope.
Once i had dreams,
they've gone up in smoke.
Once i had dreams,
Of being myself.
Now all those dreams,
Are back on the shelf.
Once i had dreams,
I hid them away.
I just knew that the world,
Wouldn't see me for me,
Once i had dreams,
And now they're all gone.
All of the dreams,
I should never have held.
Once i had dreams,
But now i'm in hell.
And looking inside,
You know I can tell.
All of my dreams,
Made my life hell.
I'm working it through,
There's no going back.
This is my life,
This is my life and it's living hell.

TRANZZII GEE
05/09/2018

BEAUTIFUL ME

I looked into my eyes,
I saw the beauty there,
I saw my raven hair,
Cascading down my form.
Raven hair,
Struck through with blue,
But none of it stopped there.
I looked into the mirror,
My soul held there for me,
And saw for all its worth,
All of what is me.
I'm the very definition,
Of what beauty is to me.

TRANZZII GEE
13/09/2018

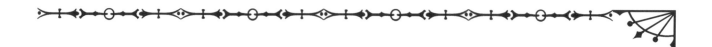

DREAMS OF MINE

Where will these dreams of mine,
Take me in the end.
Places I have never been,
See things I've never seen,
My hope is bold and promise filled,
What right have I to dream at all?
I spent a life in hells dark halls,
Atoned and purged my soul of guilt,
Existence now my right to live,
This love a right to give.
To live my life full and free,
This is just my dream for me.

TRANZZII GEE
01/09/2018

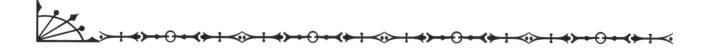

THIS MADDENING HELL

Maddening hell,
This life of mine.
Looking forward,
Looking back,
Stuck here in between,
In this maddening dream.
Get knocked down,
Upon my knees,
Round it comes again,
I see the light,
Walking now,
I struggle to edge.
Maddening hell,
Spinning round,
Shifting sand beneath my feet,
Has changed just where i stand,
Shifting sand all around,
Solid where I stand.
Looking up,
Reaching down,
Her hand I touch with mine.
My soul ignites,
Eternal flame,
I am almost home.

TRANZZII GEE
12/09/2018

WASTED LIFE

This life of waste,
Corrupted time.
I wish it at an end.
My wish to die,
Never heard,
Time has worn me down.
Toiling on,
I do not know,
Why I'm here at all.
What meaning,
No reason seen,
This game of life unplayed.
Waiting here,
Death my cure,
I wait each day to die.
A mothers touch,
Upon my heart,
My Fears are chased away.

TRANZZII GEE
10/09/2018

WHAT I LEARNED

No whispered word,
Of hope is heard.
I stand alone,
And face what's learned.
The choice is mine,
To stand and fight,
Or just lay down and die.
Pondered thoughts.
What passion brings,
To living life.
I stand alone,
And sing this song,
My song it seems,
A lonely tune,
My soul does sing for me.
Drawing nearer,
Closer still,
Each and everyday renewed,
The tune remains the same.
Find your passion,
Live your truth,
To thine own self be true.

TRANZZII GEE
09/09/2018

LIVE YOUR LIFE

When the dead of heart surround,
Hate to care,
Care to hate,
Either one,
But love will set it straight,
In the end love is all it takes.
Not lust,
Not spite,
Nor hateful words,
Nor grudges held,
All the things by ego fed,
Turn your thoughts to love instead.
Live your life as if today,
Is the last you have to live,
Yesterday is gone away,
And tomorrow's never promised,
Live for love not hateful ways,
Live a life of peace filled days.

TRANZZII GEE
09/09/2018

BUGS IN A JAR

Sadly alone,
In a world that doesnt care.
In a world where people,
Are all about themselves.
They pretend and they lie,
Protecting emselves,
From what?
Im not even sure...
But my heart just breaks,
When i see them at war….
No one it seems,
Can see who they are....
They believe its all real…
Bugs in a jar.
TRANZZII GEE
27/01/2019

As barkeep shuts and bars his door,
His whispered words they did implore.
"Dear patron hurry home".
I turned right then,
And faced the street,
And heard our doom,
The townsfolk's dread,
Out upon the moor.
Filled with dread I set about,
Surviving this nights dead.
I ran and flew,
Straight and true,
Along the pathway home.
I remember not the getting home,
But waking in my bed.

TRANZZII GEE
22/01/2019

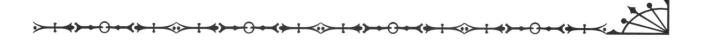

There came a time i needed you,
But you let me walk away.
I asked to stay,
But I walked away,
Now I'm on my own,
You've proven since,
That i was right.
Ill not darken you again.
I'm sorry for everything,
You think i did to you.

TRANZZII GEE
21/01/2019

you will be missed,
your heart of gold,
loved by family,
loved by friends,
loved by those you met.
you will be missed,
a hole is left,
no one else can fill.
in peace you dwell,
eternal sleep,
suffer now no more.

TRANZZII GEE
18/01/2019

what are we if we are not kind?
what are if we have no empathy?
what are we if kindness cant be found inside?
what are we if devoid of love?
if none of these are found inside,
and some require others,
then what are we deep within?
out of touch with our own spirit....

TRANZZII GEE
16/01/2019

nothing left but passion felt,
nothing left my eyes can see.
within this darkest time of mine,
held in warm embrace.
my vision gone,
of whats outside.
All has turned within.
now my mind can see your eyes,
as you're watching out for me.

TRANZZII GEE
15/01/2019

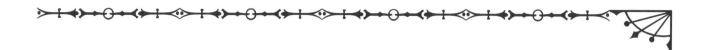

in a dream i wept and cried,
i saw what man had made and tried..
i saw the scope of evil deeds....
i wept and cried.
til anguish died,
forgiveness come undone.
i saw the blood on battlefields,
the profit made from evil deeds.
all the people left to feed.
starvation came,
as always does,
when the battles done....
then the dreamish vista changed,
I saw the world in peace and love.
i saw the people of the earth.
They lived their lives in peace and hope.
no profit made by demon hordes
no war nor hate existed there,
in this world of dreams.
i wished right then that this was now,
the wars all gone,
no humans scarred.
people lived,
No fear was known.
Just love,
and peace,
and harmony.
now dream your dream,
live it to,
we can make this world a better place,
not just for the few....

TRANZZII GEE
11/01/2019

To be reborn.
Desire torn.
Casting off the chains.
Ego born cast aside.
All my cares reside.
Past undone.
Forgiveness won.
A future now is mine.
Now reborn.
No longer torn.
That which i desire.

TRANZZII GEE
21/07/2018

I wish that i could,
Feel the whisper of your words,
Touch my heart so deeply,
That i feel the cosmos sigh.
I wish that i could,
Look into your eyes,
To see heavens spinninng there,
And see the depths of you.
I wish that i could,
Hear your voice again,
Like music never heard,
Played upon my heart.
I wish that i could,
Feel your warm embrace,
Your body pressed to mine,
Our spirits intertwine.
I wish that i could,
But im sure it cannot be,
It once felt true,
But now that truth is gone.
I wish that i could,
Not be here like this,
But what seems real to me right now,
Is ill ever be alone.

TRANZZII GEE
20/07/2018

Is it really possible,
Dreams can come true?
Pulled into what is real,
Just by what you do?
Manifested in your life,
Just by pure desire?
Is it actually possible,
That dreams can be this real?
Everything thats happening,
Seems so real to me.
Ive gone from thinking nothings real,
To something so profoundly felt..
Is it really possible,
That dreams can be this real?

TRANZZII GEE
27/07/2018.

To see her face,
Rememberance of her warm embrace,
To hear her voice again just once,
These things bring tears of joy.
To imagine the feel ofjer hand and in mine,
Brings a warmth ive never known.
To gaze into her eyes,
And maybe see...
Hidden there...
The love i also feel for her.
Dare i dream of such of a thing,
It seems impossible...
In my wildest dreams,
It seems impossible...
But what are dreams,
If not hope...
Her beauty is beyond this realm,
Dare i hope or dream?
I cannot seem to stop this dream,
Desire burns my soul.
What right have i,
To dream like this.
But still it will not stop,
No matter how i try.
My heart and soul cry her name.
What right have i to hope at all?

TRANZZII GEE
30/07/2018

WORST POEM EVER WRITTEN

No epic ode has been writ,
that can compare to this.
This ode i write,
i don't know why,
i must be bored as shit.
This ode won't say,
Wont tell me why.
It really wont say much.
By the very end.
I must be bored as shit.
I think i'm bored,
My brain it says,
It's kind of bored.
It doesn't really know.
I think i'm bored as shit.
What to do,
When bored like this.
Let's just write a poem.
My mind is strange,
When it's bored as shit.
To think i only just awoke,
For me to be this bored.
Hope it means i'm going out.
As you might guess,
I must be bored as shit.
As i promised,
By the end,
This poem would not say shit,
now i'm at the end of it,
It didn't say jackshit.

TRANZZII GEE
24/07/2018

CPSIA information can be obtained
at www.ICGtesting.com
Printed in the USA
BVHW021208020519
547197BV00005B/26/P